Growing Up in America
1830–1860

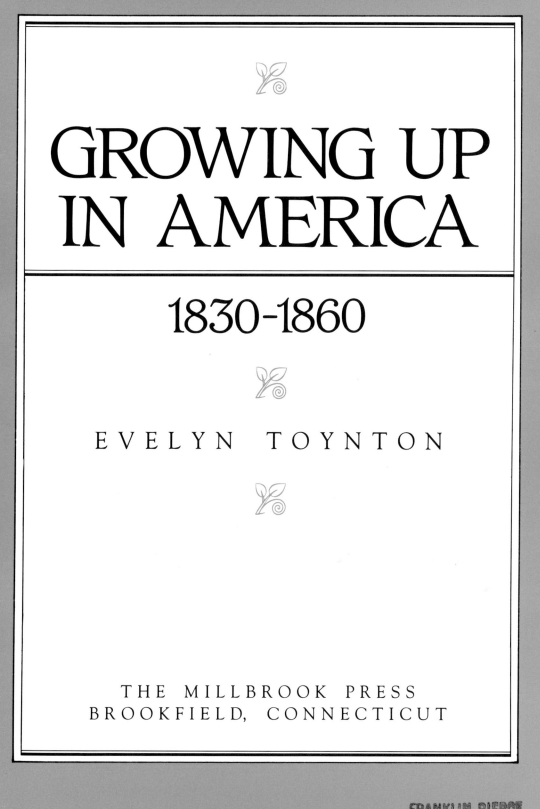

GROWING UP IN AMERICA

1830-1860

EVELYN TOYNTON

THE MILLBROOK PRESS
BROOKFIELD, CONNECTICUT

Cover: *Children of Commodore John Daniel Danels* attributed to Robert Street, photo courtesy of Maryland Historical Society, Baltimore

Photographs courtesy of The New-York Historical Society: pp. 10, 16 (bottom), 25; North Wind Picture Archives: pp. 14, 16 (top), 20, 22, 31, 43, 49, 54, 56 (top), 62, 66, 69, 72, 81; Bettmann: pp. 28, 41, 46, 75, 77; State Historical Society of North Dakota: p. 34; Historical Pictures: pp. 37, 51; New York Public Library Picture Collection: pp. 56 (bottom), 84

Library of Congress Cataloging-in-Publication Data
Toynton, Evelyn, 1950–
Growing up in America, 1830–1860 / Evelyn Toynton.
p.   cm.
Includes bibliographical references and index.
Summary: a picture of life for children growing up in the decades before the Civil War in New England, on the Plains, and in the South.
ISBN 1-56294-453-3
1. United States—Social life and customs—1783–1865—Juvenile literature.   2. Children—United States—History—19th century—Juvenile literature.   I. Title.
e165.B437   1995   973.5—dc20   94-13088   CIP   AC

Published by The Millbrook Press
2 Old New Milford Road, Brookfield, Connecticut 06804

For Daniel and Rebecca

Contents

Introduction

Have you ever wondered what it would have been like to grow up 150 years ago? Maybe you imagine yourself crossing the prairies in a covered wagon, or living in a white clapboard house on a New England farm with all sorts of animals grazing in your yard. Or maybe you see yourself riding a chestnut horse along a clean, peaceful southern river on a lazy summer day. You might think it would be fun to wear a long dress and petticoats, or a buckskin jacket, or to use candles instead of electric light. You might think, as many grown-ups tend to do, how much simpler and slower life was then and wish you could have lived in those days.

When there were no airplanes in the skies, maybe it was easier to think of them as the Heavens. When there were no movies, no televisions, no radios, people were more cut off from the world outside their own communities, but maybe they talked to each other more. Or maybe they relied on their own imaginations in ways that we've forgotten how to do.

On the other hand, what would it have been like to get sick in the 1800s, before there were medicines like penicillin and other "wonder drugs"? Children knew that many diseases could be fatal—things like scarlet fever, diphtheria,

In the mid-1800s, nature was often seen as very romantic. In this charming country scene, women and children celebrate the arrival of spring.

whooping cough, and other illnesses that have either disappeared or aren't very dangerous today. In the early years of the nineteenth century, almost a third of all children born in the United States died before they reached the age of sixteen—of disease, of minor cuts and scratches that became infected and could not be treated, and maybe just as often of the dangerous cures, such as large doses of mercury, that were tried on them by well-meaning parents and doctors. What was it like to grow up knowing that your chances were only two in three of reaching adulthood?

We can't really know what it felt like to be a child back then, but we *can* know at least some things—what toys children played with, for example, what kind of schools they went to, what books they read, what chores they did. These are the questions this book will try to answer. First, though, we'll look at what America itself was like in those days.

Despite the picture we sometimes have of it as a tranquil, unchanging world, the nineteenth century was a time of enormous change—maybe the first time in history that constant change was the norm. Much of that change was due to the industrialization that was taking hold, in this country and many others. The hundreds of scientific inventions of the age altered forever how work was done, how things were made, and how people lived.

Until about 1800, almost all Americans—97 percent, to be exact—lived in the country. In the New England villages of colonial days and after, farming and trades like blacksmithing and leatherworking and carpentry were people's main occupations. Fathers and mothers alike worked at home, and children helped out. Little girls were expected to help their mothers in the kitchen. Boys might be expected to do more of the farm chores or to help out in the carpentry or blacksmith shop. But everyone worked together on things like harvesting the crops or tending the animals.

Over the course of the nineteenth century, as factories sprang up throughout the eastern United States, more and more fathers went out to work. In 1820 about 72 percent of all American workers were on farms. By 1850 that figure had dropped to 64 percent, and it continued to decline. Mothers, too, went to work in the textile and clothing mills, if the family needed their salaries, and often whole families were employed in the same factory. But, obviously, this was not the same as everyone working together at home. And in middle-class families, mothers invariably stayed at home with the children while the fathers went out to earn the money.

For the first time, then, mothers were more of a presence in their children's lives than fathers were. Fathers spent less and less time with their children, more and more time outside the home. This was a major change in the way many children grew up in the nineteenth century. Of course there were still farms in New England, and frontier families who farmed the land all worked together in the old way. But much of the population, for the first time, lived in industrial towns or in the rapidly growing cities.

Industrialization also meant that, for the first time, there was a lot of wealth in America, and a lot of poverty, too. In colonial times, when farming was the chief occupation in the country, hardly anybody was really rich, just as hardly anybody was desperate for food or a place to live. Of course, some farmers were more prosperous than others, and those with a great deal of land could support their families in a more comfortable style. But there were very few great mansions in old New England and just as few broken-down shacks.

Industrialization changed all that. There was no comparison between the lives led by the families of factory or mine owners and the lives led by the families of factory or mine workers. Similarly, an owner of a thriving shop and someone who worked in that shop, selling buttons, for example, led wholly different lives: Their houses were different, their clothes were different, their children went to different schools and had different opportunities.

The other major factor that shaped America during this time was immigration. While there were only 300,000 immigrants to this country between 1775 and 1820, more than 2 million arrived in the course of the next twenty-five years. In the 1840s some 1.5 million people arrived. In 1849 alone, 300,000 immigrants arrived on these shores, many of them from Germany, many others from Ireland, which was undergoing a terrible famine. And in the 1850s the pace of immigration picked up still further, with 2.6 million people arriving.

A large number of the German immigrants immediately headed out west, where land could be bought at one-tenth or one-twentieth the price it cost in Europe. But just getting out west required at least some money, and most of the Irish who arrived in the United States came with hardly anything but the clothes on their backs. So instead of heading for the frontier, they tended to remain in the port cities where they had arrived, especially New York and Boston. In 1830, New York had 200,000 inhabitants. By 1850 its population had reached 515,000. In 1860 it was roughly a million—more than half of them immigrants and their American-born children.

Although America continued to attract these immigrants in such vast numbers because of the promise of a better life here, it was not always easy for them to get on their feet. And there was still a lot of prejudice against immigrants, Irish ones in particular. Since the earliest settlers had been mostly English, and since the English had always looked down on the Irish, this prejudice followed the Irish across the ocean. It was a common experience for an Irishman to go to an address where a job was offered or a room was for rent and find a sign in the window that said, "No Irish need apply." But when it came time to build the first railroads, it was the Irish who did most of the dirty and dangerous work.

A ship packed with hundreds of immigrants has docked at Rutger's Slip, New York, in the 1850s. More than seven million people came to America between 1820 and 1870; about five million were either Irish or German.

Slaveholders down south, who regarded their black slaves as valuable property, would not let them work at railroad building, because there were so many fatal accidents and so much disease brought on by unsanitary conditions and overwork in the sun. The life of an Irishman, however, was considered cheap. So it was the Irish who suffered and died to build the eastern railroads—just as, later in the century, many Chinese laborers died in the process of building the western railroads.

Yet the immigrants kept right on coming, if only because in America there was at least hope that a better life could be found. While many people wound up as poor and miserable as they had been in their native countries, there were also many who prospered.

The children of these immigrants, who had been born here or had come to America when they were very young, often found themselves caught between the customs of their parents and those of their new home. Being young and going to school with other new Americans, they adapted more quickly and became Americanized much more completely than their parents. In many cases, part of becoming American meant that they questioned and rebelled against all the values and rules and ideas their parents had brought with them from the old country. In this land of freedom, they themselves wanted more freedom than their parents were prepared to allow. After all, that was what being American was all about—not being confined by the rules and fears and restrictions of life in Europe, having a sense of limitless possibility.

So, in many cases, the parents would stay Irish or German or Swedish or Italian in their attitudes and customs, and see their children turn into Americans. They might mourn their children's lack of love and respect for the old ways, or they might be glad to see them pursuing the American dream. Either way, though, there was a "generation gap" between these immigrants and their children that was perhaps more profound than anything we see today—except among the new waves of immigrants, who often experience the same thing. Some people see this as the tragedy of immigration, others as what America is all about. In a way, every child of immigrant parents discovered America for herself or himself. Every child was an explorer in a new world.

Children at play in a barn; children gather around an organ-grinder and beg for money on a New York City street. Before cars, airplanes, radio, movies, and television, communities knew much less about each other, and ways of life were more distinct.

PART ONE

DIFFERENT WAYS OF LIFE

There were so many different ways of life in nineteenth-century America that it would be impossible to talk about all of them here. In the pages that follow, we will take a look at just a few kinds of growing-up experiences: growing up on a New England farm, for example, and growing up on the Plains frontier. We will also see what it was like to grow up poor in the big cities of America, as a member of the Sioux tribe, and as a black slave on a plantation in the South.

You can probably imagine how different all these kinds of experiences were. In fact, the differences between places and ways of life in the nineteenth century were even greater than they are today. Nowadays, poor children in Mississippi and rich children in California—or vice versa—at least see the same movies and watch the same television shows; they even wear the same kinds of clothes, such as sneakers and blue jeans. And they all go to school. A hundred and fifty years ago, though, not all children went to school, and the lives of street urchins and New England farm children—or black and white children on the same plantation, for that matter—were so completely different that they might have been living in separate worlds.

We will look at a few of those worlds in the pages that follow.

Children in
New England

First, let's see what a New England village looked like at the beginning of the nineteenth century. There would have been a village green—a large patch of lawn, shaded by trees—with several white wooden buildings clustered around it. These were the church, with its narrow spire soaring above everything else in sight, the schoolhouse, the village store, and some craftsmen's shops. There was sure to be a blacksmith's shop, where horseshoes were made in a blazing furnace called a forge, plows and other farm utensils were repaired, and all sorts of metal objects like nails and hinges were made. There was usually a metalworker's shop, where tin or pewter was also melted in a hot forge, and cooking and eating utensils were made and repaired.

Off in the distance, there would be farmhouses and barns. The average New England village in those days was made up of about 200 families, each with its own farm of 100 to 200 acres (40 to 80 hectares). Even the minister and the craftsmen usually farmed in addition to their other work.

Now let's go inside one of those farmhouses and see how the family lived. The kitchen was generally the busiest room in the house, and the warmest one too. Whereas fires in the bedrooms and the parlor might be lit only on the coldest days, a fire was kept going in the huge kitchen fireplace all the time. There, the cooking was done and the water was heated for washing; you were almost sure to find something bubbling on the heavy pot hung over the fire at any time of day.

When the children woke up at daybreak, they would come downstairs from their bedrooms, sit with their parents at the long wooden table in the kitchen, and say a prayer of thanks for the food they were about to receive. Often, the father of the family, who had probably been up for a while already, milking the cows, would read aloud to them from the Bible; if he didn't do this at breakfast, he probably did

A church, town hall, and school in Lancaster, Massachusetts, face the village green, where townspeople stroll and stop to chat.

at supper. Then everyone would have a hearty meal of homemade cheese and rye or bran bread and butter, with smoked ham or salt beef made from their own animals.

To drink, there was weak tea or weak coffee. Tea leaves and coffee beans were among the few things that farm families could not grow for themselves; such luxuries had to be bought at the village store, so the thrifty New Englanders used them sparingly. You may wonder why the family didn't drink milk, which they got for free from their own cows. But there were no iceboxes or refrigerators to keep things fresh in the hot weather, when cows gave the most milk, so milk was made into butter, buttermilk, or cheese instead of being used for drinking. Even the children of the family rarely got milk to drink.

After breakfast, there were many chores to be done both inside and out. Boys might go out to a back field to help their fathers reap the barley, spread cow manure on the cornfields (not a very nice job), or hoe the potatoes. In the spring—plowing season—they might be given the hard task of plowing the fields, with oxen hitched to the heavy old-fashioned plow. Or they might be asked to break in young oxen to accept the plow.

There were always repairs to be done and fences to build, to keep the sheep and cows from straying. The boys would help their fathers chop down trees on the part of the farm that was still wooded and then split the logs to make fence posts, all with heavy axes. Afterward they would carry the posts to the pasture that needed a fence, bore holes in the posts with an adze, and set the fences in. Building a fence around a single pasture might take three days or more—and building stone walls took even longer.

A boy takes a break in his plowing to watch a pretty girl herding a cow along the road.

On those old New England farms, much more land was given over to pasture for the animals and mowing fields for hay than to crops. On a 100-acre farm, maybe 10 acres (4 hectares) were planted with crops, and everything that was grown was for the family's own use. The potatoes would be stored in the cool ground cellar for the winter, along with vegetables from the garden and some corn. Much of the corn, however, would be ground for use in cornmeal mush and bread. Because wheat would not grow well in the Northeast, New England families made their bread out of ground corn and a little rye flour.

It was the women's and girls' job to make that bread, just

as it was their job to make butter and cheese out of the milk from the family cows. To make butter, first the milk had to be strained and set out in pans for a day or more, until the cream rose to the top; then the girl of the house could begin the hard work of churning. She had to push the wooden plunger up and down into the cream for at least a half hour before the butter formed. No wonder, if you look at paintings of farm girls, they have such sturdy arms!

Making cheese—and much more cheese was made than butter, since it lasted longer—was just as time-consuming. It involved adding rennet, made from the lining of a calf's stomach, to the milk. Rennet made the milk go lumpy, with watery liquid surrounding the lumps; the lumps were called curds and the liquid, whey (remember Little Miss Muffet?). Then the curds were strained through cheesecloth and kneaded by hand to squeeze out as much whey as possible. Finally, a wooden press was used to get rid of any remaining liquid. Then the cheese was put aside to age.

At the same time that they were making cheese, the women of the house were usually cooking something on the fire—maybe an iron pot full of pumpkins and turnips and beans and peas. These all came from the family garden, which the girls of the family were often responsible for.

Girls also helped their mothers to make candles and soap out of animal fat, and it was often their task to feed the pigs and other animals in the farmyard on scraps from the family's table. Another of their jobs was to gather the eggs from the family's hens. This was a little like an Easter egg hunt, since the hens wandered all over the yard, laying eggs wherever they happened to come to rest. Usually, the eggs were not for eating on their own but to be used in baking.

Perhaps the biggest job that the females had was to make the cloth—and then the clothes—the family needed. The average family made 100 yards (90 meters) of cloth a year, a process that involved hundreds of woman-hours of work. There were two kinds of cloth: wool and linen. The wool came from the family's sheep, which the men sheared. The linen was made from flax plants grown on the farm. Once the men had picked the flax—sometimes the women and children helped—all the seeds had to be removed with a comblike instrument, a job that fell to the women. Then the fibers had to be separated from the rough outer covering. Next the fibers had to be straightened by drawing them across a wooden board with iron teeth, and finally the spinning could begin.

Because spinning flax and wool into usable balls of yarn was such a boring, drawn-out process, the women of the village would get together to do it. Mothers and daughters would load their wooden spinning wheels into the family's oxcart and drive to a neighbor's house, where all the women would sit talking and laughing together. Sometimes these spinning bees would go on for days, with everyone drawn up close to the fireplace or to the wooden stoves that began replacing open fires in the 1830s.

Once the spinning was done, the yarn had to be wound into balls. Then it was dyed and woven on a large wooden loom. After all that came the job of turning the cloth into clothes or curtains or tablecloths or whatever the family needed. Of course, sewing had to be done by hand too. The women would get together for sewing bees or quilting bees, where they stitched scraps of cloth into bedcovers, sometimes with patterns of flowers or farm scenes on them.

When it came time to harvest crops, neighbors gathered to help each other out. New England corn-husking bees, such as this one, were a mixture of work and fun.

If the women turned their labor into social occasions, so did the men. They had house- and barn-raising bees, corn-husking bees, and stone bees, where everybody brought teams of oxen and helped clear someone's field of stones. But the high point of every summer was the haying bees, when all the men and boys of the village would help their neighbors harvest the precious hay that would feed their animals for the winter. First they would cut the hay with scythes or knives, then rake it, then spread it out to dry in the pasture. Once it was dried, they had to gather it all up, put it in neat bales (bundles), tie it with string, load it onto carts, take it to the barn, and store it for the winter. If it looked as though it might rain while the hay was still drying in the fields, they had to work at double speed to bale it and bring it in, since hay could be ruined if it got wet after being cut.

After the haying came a big feast for everyone who had helped. Lamb or beef stew, hash, plum cakes and puddings, apple pies with raisins in them, fresh cream, wild berries from the woods—all sorts of treats cooked up by the women while the men brought the hay in. After the meal, when the adults were sitting around talking, the children might make whistles out of pumpkin stalks and sit in the hayfield playing tunes on them.

Other big events in the lives of New England children were the county fairs in the autumn, where livestock would be shown and judged, with prizes awarded for the best cattle or the biggest pig. Contests would be held in plowing and horse-pulling, and traveling players might come to put on shows or to play music. While the men and boys competed in races, jumping contests, and feats of strength, the women and girls would hope to win a prize for the most beautiful quilt, the best pie, or the finest "fancywork" (embroidery).

Of course, these great fairs took place only once a year. But there were also many smaller local gatherings where young people got together—church meetings, church socials, and private dances in people's farmhouses.

Perhaps the commonest meeting place in the village, though, was the village store, where people stood and talked for hours among the balls of yarn, bolts of cloth—which only the very richest could afford to buy—and sweet-smelling barrels of spices.

Children on the Plains

From the 1820s on, wagon trains of settlers were heading to the lands west of the original thirteen states. As early as 1839, there were one hundred white settlers in western Oregon Territory, and after gold was discovered in California in 1848, the pace of immigration, especially by single men, increased rapidly. Most of the families who headed west before the Civil War, however, did not venture as far as the Pacific Coast or even the Rockies. Instead, they settled in the Great Plains region we now called the Midwest.

Taming the frontier was one of the great American adventures, and when we think of the pioneers of the nineteenth century, we think of them as very American characters. In fact, since many of them were immigrants who headed west as soon as they got off the boat, there were whole frontier settlements on the Great Plains where nothing but German or Swedish was spoken, and the customs of the old country were faithfully kept. To the first pioneers, living in the harsh wilderness, European customs represented their one link with civilization. Drawn to America by the availability of cheap or even free land—something unheard of in Europe—they were grateful to their new country but often homesick for the places they had left behind. At

A boy looks with admiration at his father who is resting after chopping down a tree. Pioneers did everything for themselves: They built their own cabins and cleared their land for farming.

Christmastime, for example, German settlers would make the traditional stollen and other German foods and have the traditional fir tree with a hand-carved angel on top in their living rooms. It was from them that other Americans adopted the custom of having a Christmas tree.

To the pioneer children of the Plains, the wilderness that surrounded them must often have seemed like paradise. Outside the little cabins where they lived with their families were miles of beautiful untouched forests or vast stretches of open prairie. The woods were full of birds and deer and other animals, wild berries and fruits grew in profusion, and fish leapt and swam in the clear cold waters of the streams. The abundance of forest in many parts of the Midwest meant endless supplies of building materials and firewood.

This paradise, however, was also full of danger: from wild animals who might attack when night came, from fast-spreading fires in the high grasses of the prairie, from fierce lightning storms in the summer and raging blizzards in the winter. Nor could frontier families on the Great Plains always rely on the animals and plants they could find to feed themselves. Through long, harsh winters there were no growing things to be found. And so the pioneers worked hard to clear the forests and prairies and plant crops. They even plowed strips of bare earth to keep prairie fires from spreading and destroying their homes.

Conditions were often far from ideal for farming. Winters were bitterly cold, and spring rains and thaw turned the ground to thick mud. And summers were hot and buggy. There was always more work to be done just to survive.

Pioneer children were very much part of the work. They hunted for mushrooms, gathered the chokeberries, elderberries, and other fruits that grew wild along the creeks, and fished. Sometimes they set traps and nets to catch small animals and birds, or hunted for the eggs of ducks or prairie chickens. They did more serious hunting too, stalking and killing antelopes, raccoons, deer, bison, and above all rabbits. Children as young as seven—girls as well as boys—were often their families' chief suppliers of meat, since grown men could not spare the time from their farm chores for hunting.

The children also worked in the fields with their parents. They plowed the fields using the new steel-tipped plows that required less strength than the old-fashioned kind, broke up the soil with knives for planting, helped to plant, and were often responsible for tending the growing crops—weeding the fields and shooing away the animals that came to steal food. At harvesttime, the whole family could be found in the fields picking the crops. Children were often responsible for planting and tending the family's vegetable gardens; girls helped their mothers to can and preserve vegetables for the winter.

In New England, neighbors and nearby relatives could be counted on to pitch in and help with the work when they were needed, but frontier families were often all on their own. That meant the children had to do a lot of work that their eastern counterparts were spared. They grew up faster and took on more responsibility than children elsewhere in the country. The spirit of self-reliance that was so much a part of the frontier was just as evident in the children as in the adults.

Much of frontier living went on outside, especially in summer, when the sun beat down on the log cabins of the settlers and made them broiling hot. Once the hot weather

A pioneer girl helps her mother by peeling apples. Children who grew up on the frontier were expected to help with daily chores from a very young age.

came, women often cooked over outdoor fires. Little girls would help their mothers prepare the food. Often, the whole family would eat outside, too. Log cabins usually didn't have too many windows, so it was impossible to cool them down even when evening came. Families would stay outside for as long as they could, fighting off flies and mosquitoes, rather than going back into their stifling homes. But they almost always slept inside their houses, for fear of being attacked by wild animals.

The clothes that pioneer children wore didn't do much to help them stay cool. Boys, like their fathers, were expected to wear heavy boots and long pants to work in the fields. And they were expected to keep their shirts on, too, even as they labored in the sun. It was considered very bad taste to go around with a bare chest.

Girls, meanwhile, had to wear long, high-necked, full dresses with at least one long petticoat and one pair of pantalettes (long cotton underwear with flounces) underneath. Like their mothers, they also wore sunbonnets and long sleeves so that they wouldn't turn brown from the sun. It was thought very unladylike to be tan. Women were supposed to look pale and delicate, even if they had to work just as hard as the men.

Pioneer families didn't get to take two weeks off in the summer, either. They had too much work do to. A trip into the nearest town, where they could visit friends and buy provisions at the general store, was like a holiday for them. And on the Fourth of July they might ride into town in the wagon and eat ices and watch the parade or the fireworks, if there were any. That was the biggest treat of all. On the Fourth of July there were no Swedes or Germans anymore; everyone was an American.

Children of the Sioux

Every Native American tribe had its own customs and practices and ways of looking at the world, although they all shared a loving respect for nature and its wonders. So it would be impossible to tell what it was like to be an "Indian" child in the nineteenth century. We can only talk about growing up as a member of one tribe or another.

Let's look at what it was like to be a child of Sioux parents. The Sioux were a nation made up of seven different tribes, living in a vast area of the Great Plains that we now call North and South Dakota. (As a matter of fact, Dakota was another name for the Sioux.) While there were thirty-one different tribes living on the Great Plains at that time, the Sioux were the largest and most famous of them. Their life was fairly peaceful during the first half of the nineteenth century—that is, before the white settlers began coming west by the thousands.

A peaceful life did not mean a settled one, however. Sioux children never grew up in one place; the Sioux moved from place to place all the time, hunting the buffalo that roamed the plains. All the people in the village would travel together from one camp to another, carrying all their belongings on travois, wooden sleds drawn by dogs or horses. The men rode on horses, with their young male children

A Sioux camp on the Great Plains in 1839. The Sioux did not bury their dead as Europeans did; they laid them out on wooden platforms, like the one pictured here.

held in front of them. Babies rode on cradles that were strapped to their mothers' backs. Only in winter months, when it was too cold to hunt and the snow-covered buffalo were hard to spot against the snow-covered landscape, did the Sioux stay in one place for long.

Each time they moved, the women of the tribe took down the tepees and then put them up again in the new camp.

Tepees were always just one room, so the whole family slept in the same space, wrapped up in soft buffalo robes that cushioned them from the hardness of the bare earthen floor. Because the strong buffalo hides from which the tepees were made were fine protection against the weather, tepees were warm in winter and cool in summer. And because buffalo robes were too warm for summer, the Sioux slept in soft deerskin robes.

The space to the right side of the tepee's entrance flap was kept for guests, so the family all slept on the left side— except for very young babies, whose deerskin cradles were hung on poles high above the floor.

Sioux children were not expected to go to school. Instead, they learned the skills they would need in their adult lives from their fellow villagers. At the time a Sioux child was born, his or her parents chose another set of parents to help care for the child. The second father would be chosen because he had some special skill to teach a boy child— perhaps he was a gifted hunter or medicine man. The second mother was expected to teach the girl child how to cook, how to make leather from elk, deer, and antelope skins, how to soften those skins and make clothing from them. Girls were also taught the art of decorating clothing with porcupine quills. And, of course, they had to know how to make and repair tepees! Sioux children spent as much time learning these things from their second parents as from their own mothers and fathers.

They also spent a lot of time with other villagers. The Sioux shared everything they had with each other, so a child who was hungry could just wander into the nearest tepee and be sure of something to eat; a child who was sleepy could go and take a nap on the right side of anyone's tepee door. And the best hunters and warriors of the tribe were expected to teach their skills to the young boys of the tribe. Both boys and girls were taught to swim and to ride horses— bareback—at a very early age. Girls as well as boys learned to kill small animals with bows and arrows, but they could never take part in the great buffalo hunts that took place whenever the scouts came back to camp with the announcement that they had found a buffalo herd nearby.

Hunting buffalo was very dangerous. A boy could get knocked over by a charging buffalo, or have his horse fall under him and find himself on the ground among stampeding animals. Fortunately, no buffalo hunt lasted long, since buffalo ran so fast that horses could not keep up with them for long. Once the men of the tribe had chased a buffalo herd for about ten minutes, the buffalo would be so far away it would no longer be possible to shoot at them with their bows and arrows. So their only catch was whatever animals they managed to bring down in those few minutes.

After the hunt, the women, who had been following behind on packhorses, would skin the buffalo, cut up the meat, and load it on their horses. They would keep the bones, the horns, and the hair of the animal too, since everything could be used to make something they needed. (Buffalo horns, for example, were used for spoons and cups.) Then, when the work was done, everyone would return to the camp for feasting and celebration. If a boy had just killed his first buffalo, his family might give him a special feast, where songs of praise would be made up and sung in his honor—but he would not be permitted to eat any of the buffalo meat himself. That was to remind him he should not ever want things just for himself. The Sioux also did not believe in killing more animals than they needed; they never hunted for sport alone.

In between buffalo hunts there was much work to be done, as children and adults alike had to help find and make what they needed to live. But there were many times when the whole tribe left off work and played games together. They played various sorts of ball games, ran races, held

These Sioux boys are playing a game of "follow my leader." Children did not go to school; they instead learned by listening to traditional tribal stories and by watching adults.

jumping and shooting contests, and played guessing games indoors when the weather was cold.

And then there were the great religious ceremonies. The Sioux believed that all of nature was alive with spirits. Earth was the mother of all the spirits, and their own mother as well. They prayed and sang and danced to show their reverence. The most famous Sioux ceremony was the Sun Dance, which took place every year and lasted for days, with much dancing and singing.

The Sioux also believed that everyone needed to seek the one special spirit that would protect them forever. When a Sioux boy was about twelve years old, he was sent to a little house, a sweat lodge, that had been built for him, where stones were heated and water was poured over them. When the house filled with steam, the boy would begin praying. Afterward, he would be taken to a place far from the village and left alone for four days and nights, without food or water. The idea was that his special spirit would appear to him in a vision. After four days he was carried back to the village and brought into the presence of the medicine man, the wisest man of the village, to tell what he had heard and seen. He described the things that had appeared in his dreams, and the medicine man then told him what his special spirit was. If the boy had seen a deer, it meant he would be able to run as fast as a deer. He would paint a deer on his shield and his tepee. He would make up songs and dances to his spirit. Then everyone in the village would celebrate his vision; afterward, he was not considered a boy anymore but one of the men.

Girls, too, had a ceremony for seeking their spirits. But girls were not expected to stay alone for four days and nights. Instead, an old woman from the village would stay with them. Girls were allowed to eat and drink during their vigil, and they did chores like chopping wood and making leather from skins. At the end of the four days, they too were taken to the medicine man to tell him their dreams. Afterward, all the women of the village would bathe and dress the girl for her feast of celebration; for such ceremonies, special clothing decorated with elk teeth, bear claws, feathers, and fur might be worn. The girl was given many presents in honor of her being ready to take her place among the women.

Children on
the Streets

Homelessness is not a new problem in our country. In the first half of the nineteenth century, the streets of the port cities where immigrants arrived by boat were the only home for many people of all ages. These were mainly people who had come to America to start a new life but could not find a job or a place to live. For years the only places such people could go were the public almshouses. These were frightening, dirty, overcrowded places where sick people and crazy people and people who were just poor were all squeezed together. The children of unlucky immigrants who could not make their way in the New World would have to live with their parents in these institutions, where they were in almost as much danger as on the streets. Or children would be abandoned by their parents and wind up in the almshouses on their own.

In those days the Calvinist religion and point of view were very strong in America. There was a widespread feeling that helping the poor was interfering with God's will, since it was thought that He had assigned everyone a certain place in life, which it was sinful to try to change. It was also felt that the poor must be to blame for their problems. If that was the case, to help them would only encourage them to

A policeman shines his lantern on two children asleep on a snow-covered doorstep. Many children were homeless, abandoned, or orphaned in the mid-1800s, and society was only beginning to find a way to save them from a life on the streets.

go on being lazy and good-for-nothing. They should be punished instead, so they would work harder and get themselves out of their mess. But, finally, it became obvious even to Calvinists that the almshouses were no place for children.

The first step taken was to establish orphanages—over fifty were established in the eastern part of the United States in the first decades of the century. Many of these orphanages were run by churches and by charities. In some, children were treated kindly and given an education so that they could go on to find a place in the world. In others, they were treated harshly, almost as harshly as slaves. They might be beaten for hardly any reason, or overworked, or underfed, or made to sleep in cold dormitories in winter.

For infants, there were places called foundling hospitals, but hardly any of the babies who wound up in these filthy, overcrowded establishments survived. Mothers who could not look after the infants they had borne would often leave them on a rich person's doorstep rather than bring them to the foundling hospitals, in the hope that the lady of the house would take pity on the helpless baby. In a very few cases this strategy worked, but most rich people would simply take the baby to the foundling hospital themselves. It was thought that the children of the poor would only inherit the vices of their parents, and since poverty was supposed to be caused by weakness of character, to take in a child would be to ask for trouble. Adoption was so rare in the nineteenth century that there were not even any laws governing it.

In 1825 a group of private citizens in New York City founded the House of Refuge, an institution intended to reform children who had been found wandering the streets or

Very few babies were adopted in the nineteenth century. Mothers who were too poor to feed their infants sometimes left them on the doorsteps of wealthy families, hoping that they would be taken in and cared for.

who had been brought into the courts for committing petty crimes. It was the first place that set out to reform children rather than just house them. The rationale was that by teaching children morals and job skills, it would be possible to keep them from turning into dangerous criminals, and thus all society would benefit.

Sixteen children, both boys and girls, were sent by the courts to live in the House of Refuge. Supposedly, they would receive an education, but in fact they were made to work for ten hours a day and spent only one and a half hours each day in the classroom. Discipline was very strict: The children were not allowed to speak to each other in the dormitories or the dining hall, and the sexes were completely segregated. Some of the children couldn't stand the harsh routine and ran away.

Despite its grim rules, however, the House of Refuge was at least a better shelter than either the almshouses or the bridges of the city, under which many homeless children slept. Soon numerous similar places were established, both in the United States and Europe, which took the House of Refuge as a model.

Because the reform institutions could not take in all the children who had been found guilty of petty crimes, many of them were sent to jail, where they lived side by side with hardened criminals. It became clear, however, that the children would come out of jail more knowledgeable about crime than before, and even the least softhearted of society's citizens began to acknowledge that this was no solution. In the 1840s magistrates began to experiment with probation for young offenders, to keep them out of the jails that had become training schools for criminals.

Beginning in 1854 a new approach was tried to the problem of orphaned and homeless children. That was the year the New York Children's Aid Society was founded. In addition to establishing hostels where the young boys who sold newspapers on the streets of New York could be decently housed and fed for a few pennies of their pay, the Society devised a program to "place out" street children in foster homes out West. Over the next two decades, 60,000 children would be placed in foster homes by the Society, which advertised widely in magazines, presenting their charges as adorable, well-mannered, innocent, sweet, and longing for a good home. The idea was that they would be so grateful to anyone who gave them a home that they would behave like angels.

Of course the problems that arose when street children from New York were sent to live with farm families in Kansas were sometimes greater than the Society wanted to admit. And some of the western foster parents were less interested in looking after children than in getting cheap labor to help them farm their vast tracts of land. In some cases children were exploited as badly in houses on the prairie as in the mills of the industrial East. But many children did find good homes and kind families to look after them. Like all the other experiments with orphaned or "problem" children, this one had mixed results.

However many institutions were founded to deal with the problem, there were never enough places for the homeless children of the cities. Throughout the century, visitors to America were horrified by the sight of ragged, thin, sad little children on city streets. Some of them sold newspapers or snacks like chestnuts and ears of corn; some of them were

A teacher holds an evening class in a New York City lodging house for newsboys — boys who had grown up on the streets and made a meager living by selling newspapers.

chimney sweeps; some of them — as young as three or four — danced to the music of organ-grinders to earn a few pennies. Many of them begged and hunted through trash for food all day, before going to sleep at night in coal bins or barrels. Perhaps not too surprisingly, a number of them also went in for stealing, setting fires, and insulting passersby. Charles Dickens, a famous English novelist who had written moving stories about the terrible plight of poor children in his native London, visited New York in the 1840s and declared that there were just as many pitiful, starving children in parts of the city as in the notorious London slums.

Unfortunately, America never produced a Dickens who brought people's attention to the desperate conditions of these children. But Dickens's stirring appeal to his readers in his account of the death of a little road sweeper in his novel *Bleak House* might just as easily have been addressed to Americans of the time (if we overlook his references to royalty, that is). This is what he wrote:

> Dead, your Majesty. Dead, my lords and gentlemen. Dead, Right Reverends and Wrong Reverends of every order. Dead, men and women, born with Heavenly compassion in your hearts. And dying thus around us every day.

Children
in Bondage

Of all the lives that children led during the early nineteenth century, the hardest to imagine are those of slave children in the South before the Civil War. In physical ways, the lives of homeless children in the cities may have been more miserable than some slave children's lives, since not every slave was cold and wet and hungry all the time. But of course the very fact of being a slave was a form of misery in itself. Even the poorest white child in the North could at least have hopes for a different, better future.

From the slave autobiographies that survive, we know that a slave child's chances of any sort of happiness were dependent on what kind of person the slave owner was (and imagine having an owner at all!). Many slave narratives—among them those by Frederick Douglass and Harriet Jacobs, two extraordinary people who became free themselves and helped others to freedom—tell of the shock it was to go from the household of a kind master or mistress to one in which the child was beaten, humiliated, and not seen as a person at all.

One of the things that both Douglass and Jacobs remained most grateful for, in speaking of their kinder mistresses, was

Slave quarters on a plantation in the South. Mothers had to work, so older relatives and neighbors cared for the babies. Children—those who were too young to work—were pretty much left on their own.

that these women taught them how to read—something that was actually against the law. It was thought, and rightly, that if slaves were literate they would begin to read and think about slavery itself in ways that could only make them understand more deeply the hatefulness of the system. Even more dangerous, knowing how to read and write would enable them to plan their escape and to survive in the world outside the plantation. Thus, teaching slave children to read was considered a blow against slavery.

In that respect, then, Douglass and Jacobs were among the lucky few. In other respects, their early lives were typical of the many black children who grew up in slavery on large southern plantations.

Such lives often began in the care of elderly slaves, too old to work in the fields, who were given the job of looking after slave babies. The babies' mothers were not allowed to take time off from their work to be with their children. Douglass's mother had to walk 12 miles (19 kilometers) at night to visit him in his grandmother's cabin in the woods, and then be back at work in the fields by sunrise. If there were no such elderly slaves on the plantation, older slave children would look after the infants. One ex-slave remembered: "Whenever the babies got to crying too much I would go and call their mothers from the field to come and feed them."

As children grew out of infancy, they would often spend their days alone together, perhaps looked after by slightly older brothers or sisters or cousins. They might simply play in the dirt outside their cabins, or hang about on the edge of the fields to be near their parents. Although being with other slaves all the time protected them in some ways from any depressing awareness of their status as slaves, it was considered very fortunate if the master or mistress took a liking to a slave child. Then the child was brought into the house to run errands, such as fetching umbrellas and coats for the master and mistress, or to do little chores. It was hoped that this meant the child would grow up to be a house slave rather than a field slave and thus not have to labor as hard.

Some enslaved children were chosen to work in the master's house or to be playmates for his children. This scene in South Carolina shows slaves who are part of the domestic life of the plantation owner.

Another position that was considered very lucky for a slave child was that of "play child." Play children were supposed both to play with and serve the children of the master. Since they spent so much time with the master's children in the master's house, they could at least be sure of being better fed and usually better treated than other slave children.

One play child has left a record of being told to sit in front of the fire and then lie at the bottom of his young master's bed, so that the little white child could warm his feet on his slave companion. But other slaves remembered that, when they were very young at least, they had no consciousness of being thought inferior to white children, and they played with them in the same way they played with their black friends. One slave remembered his relationship with the son of his master like this: "I was his playmate and constant associate in childhood. We were very fond of each other, and frequently slept in the same bed together." Significantly, this slave, too, was taught at least the rudiments of reading by his white friend.

Both among themselves and with the white children on the plantation, slave children played at marbles and various other childhood games. One favorite was sheepmeat, a kind of tag that involved one child throwing a ball of yarn at another as they ran. But they also had chores assigned to them by their parents. Many slave fathers hunted and trapped to put meat on their families' tables, and children were expected to check their fathers' traps during the day, while the men were in the fields. Or they were expected to carry water to the slaves working in the fields. At night, they might also go out hunting for raccoons, rabbits, and opossums with their fathers. They were also expected to tend the small vegetable gardens that slaves kept to help feed themselves.

As children grew older, they might be put to work in the fields, weeding and gathering bits of cotton that the adult pickers had missed. When they reached the age of twelve or so, they would be put to work looking after farm animals or assigned to "trash gangs," groups of slave children responsible for burning stumps or clearing the roadside of debris. Some young children, though, were expected to perform heavier labor. Many slave owners in Kentucky and Missouri hired out their young slaves to textile and tobacco factories, where they worked alongside adults and were expected to keep up with them.

The very worst part of slave children's lives was knowing that at any moment they could be sold away from the plantation where their families were, or that their parents themselves could be sold and sent far away. Over and over, slaves who left records of their lives told of the grief and sorrow of families being split up in this way. As awful as it was to see their parents or sisters and brothers beaten, it was even worse to see them on the auction block. In many cases slaves appealed to their masters to prevent this from happening, sometimes successfully, sometimes not. Parents would offer to work extra if the master would buy back their children, or to repay him out of whatever they were allowed to keep from their earnings working in factories. More decent masters and mistresses refused to sell any slaves unless their families were permitted to go along with them.

During a slave auction, a girl holds her mother tightly, terrified she will be sold away from her.

Perhaps partly because slaves were always conscious that their families could be broken up at any time at the will of cruel masters, there were strong ties not only among the members of immediate families but also with cousins, aunts, uncles, or adopted relatives who lived on the same plantation. Slaves looked after children whose parents had been sold away and also took care of the elderly slaves who could not work anymore.

On weekends and holidays, it was usual for these ex-
tended families to get together and eat, talk, and sing spiri-
tuals together. Sometimes, a slave who knew how to read
recited aloud to the others from the Bible, or spoke about
the meaning of Bible stories. For these festivities, children
were dressed in their cleanest clothes, bright ribbons were
tied into the little girls' hair, and the adults would urge them
to run races or have contests to see who could jump or throw
the farthest. Such gatherings remained the happiest memo-
ries that many slaves had of their childhoods.

Pioneer girls are on the run with a wagon outside their sod house on the prairie; city girls in elegant dresses at play with a balloon, hoop, and jump rope.

PART TWO

DAILY ACTIVITIES

So far, we have mostly looked at how children lived within their families and with their neighbors. Now we will explore what their lives outside the home were like—at school, at work, at play with friends. We will also see what kinds of toys and games and books they entertained themselves with.

Of course, the Sioux children and the slave children and the orphans who lived on the streets of the city did not go to school. Nor did they have the kinds of toys or books that will be described in the pages that follow. We will be talking, then, about the New England children and the frontier children discussed earlier.

In addition, much of what follows applies to middle-class city children and the children of the rich, both in the North and in the South. They did not have to go out to work, but they did go to school—and they certainly played games and read books. It is these children who look out at us from the portraits of the period, holding their dolls or sitting on their rocking horses, dressed in their Sunday best.

Children
at School

The first free schools for children in America were established in Philadelphia as early as 1787. Based on the Quakers' church-related schools in both England and Pennsylvania, they taught not only reading and writing but even German to those students who wanted to learn it. They also taught needlework, knitting, and spinning to the girl students.

Meanwhile, practically every New England village had its own small school, supported by modest fees that parents paid to the schoolmaster, who was often the local minister. These schools, which were closed during the planting and harvest seasons so the children could help their parents on the farm, taught basic skills like reading, writing, and "sums"—what we now call arithmetic.

During the middle part of the century, there was a massive effort to establish a good public school system that would not be connected to any religion. Horace Mann of Massachusetts campaigned vigorously for free public education for everyone, and succeeded in having laws passed in the 1830s providing for taxpayer-supported schools in many northern states. Even once a free school was established, however, getting students to attend on any sort of regular basis could be a real problem in rural areas, where most children had work to do on their parents' farms and the population was very thinly scattered. Well-to-do city parents, on the other hand, often didn't like to send their children to public schools, because they thought they might come into contact with the sort of child who would be a bad influence. Meanwhile, the parents of poor children often felt suspicious of the whole idea of education, especially if they couldn't read and write themselves. So they would keep their children at home, saying they needed them there.

Many parents hated to send their children to school at all, just because it was often such an unpleasant experience. Children had to sit for long hours on hard, backless benches, and schoolmasters were not always the kindest people. Taking for their maxim the line from the Bible about sparing the rod and spoiling the child, they used birch or hickory rods to hit naughty or slow students on the hands or the backside. "We called our Master 'Big Cane,' for the frequent use he made on us of the hickory ruler," wrote one New Englander, looking back on his schooldays. Boxing students' ears was also very common. And slow or backward students were made to sit in a corner wearing a "dunce cap."

Another problem at this time was that many of the New England schools were housed in leaky, cold buildings. That was because expenses for running a school were paid by taxing property-owners, and the thrifty Yankee farmers often resented the idea of having to pay for children's education. They would try to build the school as cheaply as possible — and to hire the cheapest possible teacher. It's no wonder that many of these teachers were hardly qualified for their work; some of them could barely read and write. Nor is it surprising that one minister who was also a congressman described most schooling in his day as "torture rather than instruction." That was the view of many students, too!

Later in the century, however, this situation improved greatly, until, in the 1880s, one observer remarked, "The most significant fact in this world today is that in nearly every village under the American flag, the schoolhouse is larger than the church."

As time wore on, the public school system expanded to include more and more students, although as late as 1860 only one out of every six American children attended school. Except in the city, the schools themselves were still usually the sort of one-room schoolhouses that have become the stuff of American legend. Here the job of teaching students who ranged from three or four years old to sixteen or even older was taken on by a single schoolmaster or schoolmistress. (Starting in the late 1820s, more and more schoolteachers were women, partly because men would not accept the low pay.)

Students were not divided up into grades, as they are now. It was simply a matter of how far advanced they were in their studies, and since many of them had to stay home and work on the harvest, they might be far behind for their age. They all worked on the same subject at the same time, but they used different books. The first reader taught the letters of the alphabet and used pictures to help students learn simple words. After the alphabet lessons came very short stories. Students learned to read with expression by reading aloud. The more advanced readers might present facts about geography or offer lessons in behavior, with quotations from the Bible about honoring your father and

School children line up to recite aloud. Other students are listening, talking, or reading in the back of the room.

mother and loving your neighbor as yourself. Bible stories were also used to instruct students in reading.

In addition to these moral lessons, pupils were expected to learn patriotic values. They would memorize the Declaration of Independence and passages from the Constitution and be asked to recite dates from American history by heart. Often, these were learned not from books, which were in short supply, but from teachers, who recited them to students until they could recite them back. Toward the middle of the century, however, more schoolbooks were introduced into the classroom, and education became a more sophisticated matter. Readers and spellers became more amusing, with lessons offered in verse, and sea stories or nature stories were used to teach students to read. History books for children also became available. But it was still considered a big part of education to recite aloud to the class—whether poetry, passages from the Bible, or stirring stories of heroes of the American Revolution. People who attended these schools often remembered those poems and stories for the rest of their lives.

The teacher in the one-room schoolhouse worked with one or two pupils at a time. While she worked with these pupils, the others were expected to study on their own or to help one another. As you can imagine, it was not always easy to keep order in such a schoolroom. A painting from 1852, called *New England School,* shows two older students kissing behind the teacher's back, while she is instructing some younger pupils. Another boy is curled up under a desk, reading, while other students chat and laugh in the back of the room. Not much learning seems to be going on. Yet very few pupils emerged from these schools unable to read and write.

Schools in the frontier settlements were similar to New England schools, except that they often lacked even the supplies the New England one-room schoolhouses had. In New England the children wrote on slates (little blackboards) that could be easily erased, while the teacher wrote on the sort of big blackboard at the front of the classroom we still have today. In frontier schools, slates might be scarce, so students would have to share them, and at times they had to write on the dirt floor of the schoolroom itself. Maps, globes, blackboards, and other teaching aids common in the New England schools were often lacking.

Like the rural schools of New England, the schools for pioneer children were open only from November, when the harvest was over, until the spring plowing and planting season. Then they opened again in summer. But the older pupils—especially the boys—who had to work in the fields might not be able to attend in the summer either. And they often skipped school in the winter, too, if there was farm work to do. Nor was there any set time for beginning and ending studies; it was up to the parents to decide when their children were educated enough.

Teachers in one-room schoolhouses had a hard life. They often had to chop the wood for the school's stove, get up early to start the fire every morning, and oversee all the different students' different levels of work. In frontier schools they were paid only about ten dollars a month at best, sometimes as little as four dollars a month. Most teachers did not have homes of their own, but boarded with the families of students, moving from family to family during the school year. It could be a lonely existence. There also continued to be many small church schools and private schools. These, having more teachers and smaller classes, could offer instruction in a greater range of subjects including not just reading, writing, and arithmetic but also foreign languages, music, drawing, dancing, and navigation—for those boys who wanted to go to sea.

In the rapidly growing cities the public schools were seen as especially important, since they were the only institution that could give children of immigrants from all over the world a common introduction to American values. For that reason, public education was approved of by most voters in all the major cities after the first few decades of the century, and funds for them increased.

America was also the first country to treat boys and girls almost equally in its schools—part of its commitment to democracy. A shocked Frenchman, visiting the United States in the middle of the century, said, "The first impression of the stranger is that there are no sexes in the United States. Girls and boys walk to school side by side, they sit on the same benches, they have the same lessons, and go about the streets alone."

Yet girls weren't really treated the same as boys: For one thing, they could not go on to college in the early part of the century, since no college accepted women. And even the wealthiest among them were not encouraged to study the Latin and Greek classics, as the boys did. In the nineteenth century one could not be called truly educated without a knowledge of Latin and Greek. These, being the basis for all Western civilization, were the foundation for all college study and considered the hallmark of the educated and civilized man. Thus the sons of the rich or the near-rich were sent to private academies, where they were drilled in Greek verbs and taught to write Greek and Latin compositions, studied higher mathematics, and introduced to great literature. Only the graduates of such academies could go on to college.

Girls' academies, meanwhile, for the daughters of the wealthy, were expected to teach deportment (manners and

Even though girls went to school in the nineteenth century, there were no women's colleges. Lessons were aimed at learning social graces rather than difficult subjects such as Latin or Greek.

good posture), music, drawing, dancing, needlework, and a smattering of French, Italian, and academic knowledge— just enough to make a female "cultivated," as the expression went. And in the case of the very rich, particularly in the South, tutors might be brought in to teach female children these subjects in their own homes. The daughter of a plantation owner in Louisiana, looking back on her childhood, remembered:

> At White Castle there were at different times teachers of several nationalities—a German master for music, who came several times a week; a French master for teaching the Terpsichorean art [dancing], who came for a month at intervals; and an English governess. . . . There were schools in New Orleans where music and French were easily acquired, as well as beautiful manners, and the young ladies of a family were frequently sent there after being grounded at home.

Yet there were some female educators who refused to limit their students' education to this fare. At the beginning of the century, Miss Sarah Pierce opened a school in Litchfield, Connecticut, where girls studied history, geography, arithmetic, and even chemistry. And Miss Emma Willard opened a school in Troy, New York, which tried to make up for the fact that girls could not go to college by offering college-level courses in mathematics and the sciences similar to those in boys' schools. In 1833, Oberlin College in Ohio became the first college to admit both men and women. In 1837 a college-level institution for women only was founded in South Hadley, Massachusetts, by Mary Lyon. Called the Mount Holyoke Female Seminary, it is still in existence today (as is Oberlin), but it is now known as Mount Holyoke College.

Children
at Play

Nineteenth-century children who posed for their portraits are often shown holding—or sitting on—a favorite toy. In these paintings and photographs we see little boys with rocking horses, hoops, toy guns, toy wagons, and all sorts of other playthings. But if the child being painted was a girl, we are almost sure to find her holding a doll. While very young boys were also given dolls to play with, they were expected to outgrow them at an early age and go on to other things. Girls, on the other hand, were encouraged to play with dolls until they were almost old enough to have their own children.

Some of these dolls were simple rag affairs, usually made at home, with black buttons for eyes and funny round cloth faces. The children of the poor, or those who lived in the country, might never see any other kind. But for middle-class or rich children, there were much more sophisticated dolls, often imported from England—beautiful china or wax creatures dressed in elegant silk dresses and the coral jewelry that was so popular for children as well as their playthings. (In fact, coral was said to prevent children from getting colds and other illnesses.) Toward the middle of the century, American factories began producing dolls in vast num-

This Christmas morning in the 1860s looks a lot like a Christmas morning today. By the mid-nineteenth century, factories were starting to produce machine-made toys that replaced the hand-made ones children had always played with.

bers, so that it was no longer necessary to import them from abroad, and more and more children could afford them. There were also many other playthings connected with dolls—doll furniture, tiny tea sets, and of course dollhouses. And paper dolls were very popular, too, just as they are today.

Another pastime that was considered just the thing for little girls was embroidery. They were taught by their mothers at an early age to make small, neat cross-stitches, which they practiced on "samplers" featuring the alphabet and different birds and animals. Girls were also expected to learn more practical forms of sewing, so that they could darn socks and help their mother make clothes for the family. But embroidery was looked on as a form of "feminine accomplishment" that every nicely brought-up daughter should learn. Many portraits of nineteenth-century girls show them bent over their embroidery hoops.

If girls were expected to amuse themselves quietly indoors with their pretty dolls and their samplers, boys were allowed to be much louder, rougher, and more active. Indeed, there were many more types of playthings for boys than for girls. A lot of them were military—not only the toy guns mentioned above but toy swords, toy cannons, toy bugles, and endless varieties of tin soldiers, with the uniforms of different regiments painted on. Marbles and tops were always very popular, and later in the century mechanical toys were all the rage. Then there were rocking horses, toy wagons, toy wheelbarrows, and all sorts of toys for boys to ride or pull or drag along. Many boys were given pony whips, too, with which to urge on their rocking horses or their make-believe horses. And, of course, many country boys went riding on real horses, as did the rich children of the city. Horses gripped the imagination of nineteenth-century children in the same way that cars and trucks are so big a part of the play of children today.

In addition, boys were encouraged to go fishing, to ride bicycles, and to play all sorts of ball games—trapball and rounders, two forerunners of baseball, were big favorites. And just as they do today, boys in the nineteenth century went in for playing war games, building treehouses, climbing fences, having contests with their friends to see who could jump highest or run farthest, and exploring any woods or countryside near where they lived. Country boys learned to shoot all sorts of small birds and animals with their bows and arrows. When they got older, these boys were taught to hunt with flintlock rifles, which usually took five or six pulls of the trigger before they went off. Such active outdoor play was seen as healthy and normal for boys, while quiet, "lady-like" play indoors was supposed to be the only appropriate kind for girls. Indeed, exercise for girls was so frowned on that various visitors from England during the course of the century commented on the sickly, pale look and frequent illnesses of middle-class American girls, and advised that they get more exercise in order to enjoy better health.

Not all American girls remained indoors playing with their dolls, though. Rolling hoops was an approved and very popular form of light exercise for both sexes, something that both city and country children could do. Jump rope, which had started as a boys' game, soon became associated with girls. Blindman's buff, a form of hide-and-seek in which the

Although girls were encouraged to stay indoors and play quietly with dolls or sew or play the piano, some, like this little girl, preferred to go fishing with the boys.

seeker was blindfolded and had to run after the other players until catching one, was also a game that both sexes enjoyed. And boys and girls both went in for sleigh rides and kite-flying, and long hours spent on swings.

In fact, quite a few tomboys among girl children managed to ignore society's rules and play catch, jump fences, or even play at soldiers. One little girl wrote in her diary in 1841 that her favorite form of play was having wrestling matches with her girlfriends! And girls were even known to play mumblety-peg, a popular, dangerous game in which some-one put a jackknife as far down in the ground as it would go, and the other player tried to get it out with his or her teeth.

A little later in the century, just after the Civil War, Lou-isa May Alcott would write about a tomboyish girl named Jo March in *Little Women* and other novels for the young. Jo immediately became the most beloved American heroine in children's literature. Obviously, many little girls must have had a streak of the tomboy in them!

In addition to games like checkers and dominoes, which could be played by both boys and girls, building blocks and jigsaw puzzles were popular. These were thought to be better for children than mere playthings, since they had some edu-cational purpose. And there were also educational playing cards, which taught simple geography, spelling, and other subjects.

Of course, there were no movies or television back then, and very few children were lucky enough to be taken to the theater more than once or twice a year. But many children put on plays for their own amusement, either written by themselves or by others. They would dress up in grown-up clothes, set up chairs in the parlor, and invite their friends and relatives to come and watch them. Or they might recite poetry to their audience, or sing or play the piano. Piano playing was another accomplishment that middle-class girls were encouraged to acquire. Often, the whole family would gather around the piano and sing popular or patriotic songs together. Or the grown-ups would tell stories, sometimes scary ghost stories, around a flickering fire.

Children at Work

As we have seen, at the beginning of the nineteenth century most people in America worked on farms. But quite a few farmers also had other trades—they were carpenters or wheelwrights or metalworkers or blacksmiths. Then there were "journeymen," who did not own their own shops or forges but were employed for wages by other craftsmen.

How did someone learn a craft? There were no trade or vocational schools where people could learn to make horseshoes at the open forge, or pour liquid pewter into molds to form mugs and plates. Instead, young boys were apprenticed to a master craftsman for a period of five to seven years in order to learn his trade. They might begin by sweeping the floor and handing the craftsman his tools, or selling his wares from farm to farm. Then, gradually, they would progress to being allowed to pour pewter or do simple carpentry. Most of what they learned, they learned from watching experienced workmen. If they proved skillful, they would be allowed to do more and more complicated tasks. Finally, they could expect to become journeymen themselves. And if they worked hard, saved their money, and had a bit of luck, eventually they would be able to open their own shops and work for themselves when they got older.

Boys working at a shoemaking factory. By 1860 only a few states had passed laws against children under the age of ten or twelve working at this kind of labor.

Apprentices were not paid for their work, but they received food, clothing—including the special caps that marked them as apprentices—a place to live, and a certain amount of education. The education of apprentices was taken very seriously: In Massachusetts, for example, any master who was illiterate and so could not teach his apprentices to read and write was required by law to send them to school. In Philadelphia and New York, night schools were established for apprentices whose masters were not qualified to teach them.

But increasingly, as the century got older, more and more

people worked in factories. The textile factories and shoe factories and other manufacturing places of the early nineteenth century were staffed mainly by two kinds of workers: women and children. Since the machines often made physical strength unnecessary, it was possible for even a young child to be put to work. In some factories, laborers were hired in family units. By the early 1820s about half of the cotton textile workers in the spinning mills of New England were under sixteen years of age.

To most people of that time, it did not seem wrong for children to be put to work: After all, children had always labored with their parents in the fields of the family farms. These same middle-class children—particularly girls—now began to work in mills. In the first part of the century the conditions in these mills were not always harsh, and the work pace was not expected to be too fast. Furthermore, the mill owners often provided some education to their child laborers, buying them English grammars, dictionaries, psalm and hymn books, and school Bibles, and bringing in teachers to offer classes.

In factories like the famous Lowell mills in Lowell, Massachusetts, young women who had come from farms all over New England lived together in clean company boardinghouses, published their own magazine, attended evening classes sponsored by the mill owners, and managed to save about half of their three-dollar weekly wage to buy the household goods they would need when they got married or to pay for a brother's education. To many of them, working seventy hours a week, which we would consider unbearable, was like easy living after the nonstop labor of farm life. Having even a few hours of leisure a day was a great luxury in

These girls, whose faces look aged beyond their years, are working in a twine factory. Not until 1938 was a law passed that restricted the amount of work an American child under the age of sixteen could do.

their eyes. And several English observers commented on how much better the conditions were in these American mills than in the English ones; they also remarked how much healthier and better dressed the American workers seemed.

Nevertheless, working in a mill was certainly no paradise, and in some of the cotton mills run by less humane owners, children as young as four labored from sunrise to sunset six days a week, with two or three days off a year. The wages of children between six and sixteen in these factories and in the weaving and glovemaking industries were half those of grown women. Similarly, low wages and much less healthy working conditions were the lot of the many children who worked in mines.

Later in the century, conditions in even the more pleasant mills changed, until they were almost as bad as in England. The pace of the machines themselves became much faster, which meant the workers had to work harder to keep up, and dust and dirt were everywhere. At the same time, more competition made factory owners try to lower their costs in order to keep their profits high. Also, the tide of immigrants meant that there were more and more people looking for work, so owners were free to offer lower salaries. By 1835 a Paterson, New Jersey, factory employing six hundred children under the age of sixteen paid them from $.50 to $1.75 a week. They had only half an hour off for breakfast and three quarters of an hour for dinner.

Meanwhile, in the cities, poor children might be sent to work when they were only three years old. Whole tenement families would do "piecework" at home, which meant anything from sewing to sorting feathers to stripping tobacco leaves. Or the children would do the same sort of work in dirty, dimly lighted sweatshops, working twelve hours a day without a single break. If they fell asleep at their work, cold water would be thrown in their faces to wake them up. (This was still less cruel than the practice in English mills of beating children who slowed down at their work.) Pieceworkers were paid according to the amount of work they produced, and rates of pay were so low that many of them who worked at home had to put in even longer hours than those in factories just to pay for rent and food.

Other children of the urban poor worked as newsboys or match sellers, spending long hours on the cold streets trying to sell their wares.

Not until much later in the century were laws passed that limited the hours a child could be asked to work. While there was pressure to adopt a ten-hour day from the 1830s on, and a few employers agreed to this, many refused. In 1847, New Hampshire was the first state to pass a ten-hour-day law. Gradually, over the next few decades, other states followed. But conditions in the larger factories in particular—not to mention the mines—were so bad that many other reforms were needed before workers were treated fairly. Not until well into the twentieth century were these reforms passed into law.

Children Reading

Although a popular children's book, the *New Gift for Children,* had been written by an American and published here as early as the 1760s, most books for children in the first years of the nineteenth century still came from England. Except for the *Mother Goose* rhymes, which first appeared in England in the 1700s and were reprinted over and over in America during the next hundred years, children's books of the time were usually either tales from the Bible or moral stories about the importance of being honest, obedient, God-fearing, and hard-working.

In many of them, terrible things happen to any child who behaves badly. In a book called *My Mother's Grave,* for example, a little girl refuses to bring her sick mother a glass of water. By the time she starts to feel bad about it and goes to say she's sorry, her mother has died. Another book, called *Vice in Its Proper Shape,* tells of a greedy little boy being turned into a pig as punishment, and a gossipy little girl waking up as a magpie (a bird that chatters all the time). Other moral tales were presented in poetry. Two English sisters, Ann and Jane Taylor, wrote many volumes of "improving" verse for children, but they are best remembered as the authors of "Twinkle, twinkle, little star."

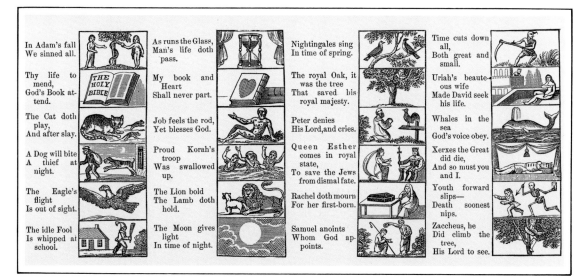

This is a page from the New England Primer, *published in 1811. Children learned the alphabet and some very somber lessons at the same time.*

Most books for children during the first half of the century were "chapbooks"—tiny paperbacks published on cheap paper. After the 1820s many of these books were produced in America, although they were often just reprinted versions of English stories. Some chapbooks, known as primers, taught the alphabet, with each letter illustrated by a bird or animal whose name started with that letter: "A is for Ape," began *The American Primer,* one of the first home-grown primers, published in 1813. Later primers were more imaginative. *Tom Thumb's Picture Alphabet,* for example, was filled with comic drawings and funny rhymes.

Various chapbooks taught small readers about geography or the glories of nature, while others told stories about incredibly good little children who suffered many trials without ever losing their virtue. *Goody Twoshoes,* another English import, is a fine example of this type. Orphaned at a young age and forced to make her way in the wide world,

Goody never loses her faith or her willingness to give advice to the other children she meets. She not only goes from house to house teaching youngsters to read, but she also shows them how to lead their lives properly. Reading the book today, it's hard to believe that none of the children she meets ever tells her to be quiet. She is always saying such things as, "Therefore, play, my dear children, and be merry; but be innocent and good. The good man sets death at defiance, for its darts are only dreadful to the wicked." In the end she marries a rich nobleman and lives happily ever after.

Other books tried to show children the evils of war, in the hopes that when they grew up they would work to bring peace into the world. Still others warned children about the dangers of drinking or spoke of the horrors of slavery. Then there were tales of animals and their adventures, biographies of great people throughout history, and books of games and riddles.

Another popular form of children's literature in the first part of the century was the travel tale, in which a boy or girl was taken on a trip and learned about the history and customs of a strange place. There was a whole series of books about a boy named Rollo, who traveled all over the world, learning moral as well as history lessons wherever he went. There were also books describing life on the frontier, or among the Indians, or in some of the great cities of America. Then there were novels-in-letters, in which a hero or heroine traveling far from home wrote long letters to family or friends describing the journey. These books were designed to teach not only geography but also the art of letter-writing, which girls in particular were expected to master.

Children were introduced to the great classics of literature in books like *Tales from Shakespeare,* published by Charles and Mary Lamb in the early 1800s. This famous English brother-and-sister team wrote some charming children's versions of old myths and fairy tales, too, as well as lovely stories about their own childhoods. (Tragically, Mary suddenly went insane and murdered their mother; Charles, who also wrote some wonderful books for adults, looked after her for the rest of her life.) Later in the century, America's own Nathaniel Hawthorne, author of the great novel of Puritan New England *The Scarlet Letter,* retold the ancient Greek myths for children in *A Wonder Book* and *Tanglewood Tales.*

In the 1820s a wonderful book of fairy tales was printed in the United States. Translated from the German, these old stories and legends had been collected by the Brothers Grimm, who wandered through Germany, listening to the folktales the countryfolk had been telling around the fireside for generations, and wrote them down for the first time. Thus, American children were introduced to the stories of Hansel and Gretel's adventure with the wicked witch, Cinderella and her glass slipper, Rapunzel and her golden hair, and many others that are still popular today. The book's original title in America was *Household Tales*—a very appropriate name, since practically every home in America where children's books were read at all soon had a copy.

About twenty years later, Hans Christian Andersen's collection of fairy tales was also translated into English and published in America. Within a short time, the stories of the little mermaid, the snow queen, the ugly duckling, Thumbelina, and the emperor's new clothes had captured the imagination of American children, as they had of Dan-

These nineteenth-century illustrations are from the story of Hansel and Gretel by the Brothers Grimm.

ish children before them. Many of Andersen's tales had their roots in Danish folklore, but many others were his own original creations. Andersen was a more gentle writer than the Brothers Grimm. Although his stories show the cruelty and sorrow of the world, they are full of a tenderness that makes them less frightening than some of the Grimms' monsters.

Perhaps the first children's book written in English that didn't preach virtue or try to teach its readers anything was Edward Lear's *Book of Nonsense,* published in his native England in 1846 and in America a few years later. Its limericks and silly verse-stories are still read and enjoyed today. Later *Nonsense Books* told of the Owl and the Pussycat, the Yonghy-Bonghy-Bo, and the Pobble who has no Toes. As the popularity of Lear's books grew, many other lighthearted books for children began appearing, usually with comical drawings like Lear's, although his are still among the best.

A Final Note

After the Civil War the lives of many American children changed dramatically. Fewer and fewer children were living on the kind of small family farms in New England we have described here. The lives of Sioux children were changed forever by the settlers who claimed much of what had been Sioux land and pushed them onto reservations. Slave children in the South were freed. Even the lives of Plains frontier children became different. As more and more people headed for the frontier, new settlers moved closer to each other, and what had once been small settlements grew into towns. There were more stores, because there were more people with things to buy and sell. Railroads made an enormous difference, too. Settlers could buy things directly from stores in the East rather than having to make everything for themselves. And new farming equipment meant that frontier farmers, like those in New England and elsewhere, could produce food for sale as well as for their own families.

The cities grew even faster, of course, especially as new waves of immigrants arrived from Europe. After the Civil War these immigrants came in large numbers not just from Germany and Ireland and other countries in western and central Europe, but from eastern Europe, too. Poles and Russians, and Jews who had been cruelly persecuted in Poland and Russia, sailed to the New World on crowded ships to find freedom and opportunity. The character of the cities changed as these new immigrants brought their customs and ways of life with them. The public school system expanded to make room for them all. At the same time, the plentiful supply of cheap labor provided by the newcomers often meant that factory and mine and mill owners could offer still lower wages and worse working conditions without ever running out of workers. In the end, things became so bad for workers that they began to fight back, and the labor unions were born.

In the years following the Civil War, the freed blacks in the South struggled to be treated with dignity and fairness. Their fight against injustice, however, did not really bring results until the twentieth century. Only in the 1960s did blacks begin to be granted equal status and opportunities. Their struggle is still going on—as is the struggle of the American Indians, who are only now beginning to reclaim some of their sacred lands from the federal government.

Children's lives change with the world around them. They have no say in these matters. Yet they are greatly affected.

Seeing how children—black, immigrant, Indian, urban, and rural—lived a long time ago is a way to understand what America used to be and, in contrast, what it is now.

Perhaps, after reading about these different growing-up experiences and comparing them with those of the present time, you will find yourself imagining how the world will have changed by the time you are ready to raise children of your own.

Further Reading

Bernheim, Marc and Evelyn. *Growing up in Old New England.* New York: Crowell-Collier Press, 1971.

*Blos, Joan W. *A Gathering of Days: A New England Girl's Journal, 1830–32.* New York: Charles Scribner's Sons, 1979.

Blumberg, Rhoda. *The Great American Gold Rush.* New York: Bradbury Press (Macmillan), 1989.

Freedman, Russell. *Children of the Wild West.* New York: Ticknor & Fields, 1983.

Freedman, Russell. *Cowboys of the Wild West.* New York: Ticknor & Fields, 1985.

Loeb, Robert H., Jr. *New England Village: Everyday Life in 1810.* Garden City, N.Y.: Doubleday & Co, 1976.

McGovern, Ann. *If You Lived with the Sioux Indians.* New York: Four Winds Press, 1972.

Osborn, Mary Pope. *American Tall Tales.* New York: Alfred A. Knopf, 1991.

Place, Marian J., & the Editors of American Heritage. *Westward on the Oregon Trail.* New York: American Heritage, 1962.

*This is a fictional account of a New England girlhood, presented in diary form.

Bibliography

Ailenroc, M. R. *The White Castle of Louisiana*. Louisville, Ky.: John P. Morton & Co., 1903.

Arbuthnot, May Hill. *Children and Books*. Chicago: Scott, Foresman & Co., 1947.

Bode, Carl, ed. *American Life in the 1840s*. New York: New York University Press, 1967.

Cable, Mary. *The Little Darlings: A History of Child-Rearing in America*. New York: Charles Scribner's Sons, 1975.

Calvert, Karin. *Children in the House: The Material Culture of Early Childhood, 1600–1900*. Boston: Northeastern University Press, 1992.

Coit, Margaret L., and the Editors of Life. *The Growing Years*. Volume 3 of the *Life History of the United States*. New York: Time Inc. Book Division, 1963.

Coit, Margaret L., and the Editors of Life. *The Sweep Westward*. Volume 4 of the *Life History of the United States*. New York: Time Inc. Book Division, 1963.

Davidson, Marshall B. *Life in America*. Volume I. Boston: Houghton Mifflin Co, 1951.

Garraty, John A. *The American Nation: A History of the United States to 1877*. Volume 1. New York: Harper & Row, 1983.

Georgiou, Constantine. *Children and their Literature.* Englewood Cliffs, N.J.: Prentice-Hall, Inc. 1967.

Glover Bicentennial Committee. *History of the Town of Glover, Vermont.* Printed by Queen City Printers, Burlington, 1983.

Hunt, Gaillard. *Life in America One Hundred Years Ago.* New York: Harper & Brothers, 1914.

Jacobs, Harriet A. *Incidents in the Life of a Slave Girl.* (Edited by L. Maria Child. Introduction by Jean Fagan Yellin.) Cambridge: Harvard University Press, 1987.

Kiefer, Monica. *American Children Through their Books: 1700 to 1835.* Philadelphia: University of Pennsylvania Press, 1948.

Owens, Leslie Howard. *This Species of Property: Slave Life and Culture in the Old South.* New York: Oxford University Press, 1976.

Rose, Willie Lee, ed. *A Documentary History of Slavery in North America.* New York: Oxford University Press, 1976.

Schorsch, Anita. *Images of Childhood: An Illustrated Social History.* New York: Mayflower Books, 1979.

Shaw, Janet. *Kirsten Saves the Day.* Madison, Wis.: Pleasant Co., 1988.

Somerville, C. John. *The Rise and Fall of Childhood.* Beverly Hills, Calif.: Sage Publications, 1982.

Tannenbaum, Frank. *Slave & Citizen: The Negro in America.* New York: Vintage Books, 1946.

Tunis, Edwin. *The Young United States: 1783 to 1830.* New York: Thomas Y. Crowell Co., 1969.

West, Elliott, and Paul Petrik, eds. *Small Worlds: Children and Adolescents in America, 1850–1950.* Lawrence: University Press of Kansas, 1992.

Index